Obedience is

Not an Option

Obedience is Not an Option

by Brian Ohse

Christian Literature & Artwork
A BOLD TRUTH Publication

Obedience is Not an Option
Copyright © 2016 by Brian Ohse
ISBN 10: 0-9972586-6-7
     13: 978-0-9972586-6-0

First Edition

Printed in the United States of America

Bold Truth Publishing
300 West 41st
Sand Springs, Oklahoma 74063
www.BoldTruthPublishing.com

10 9 8 7 6 5 4 3 2 1

Table of Contents

Author's Preface ....*i*

Obedience...1

Obedient...35

Note from the Publisher

"I want to share with you about my friend and brother in ministry, Rev. Brian Ohse. Brian was referred to our publishing company by an aquaintance who had attended one of our monthly Ministers Fellowships. We met for lunch and discussed his forthcoming book(s), the Ministry Call, The Bible and things of The Spirit, etc...

Before leaving the restaurant I watched as he ministered to the couple sitting behind us through prophecy and prayer. Our GOD IS AMAZING and Brian's heart is to hear clearly what THE HEAVENLY FATHER IS SAYING and doing in these last days.

I have to say in this modern vast desert of 'want-a-be ministries' visiting with Brian that day and watching him share God's love for that couple with no 'agenda' other than THE LOVE OF CHRIST; was a breath of Holy Ghost fresh air.

The Prophetic Call is strong in Brian's life and he does his upmost to walk that out daily. I have watched him flow in compassion toward others, with accuracy, with NO FEAR and no 'self-promotion' whatsoever; always preferring others above himself (often to his own hurt.)

I know many times he has been misunderstood, his mannerisms taken out of context or his version of casual being a 3 piece suit and tie, perceived as religious. But to him it is pure, it's about RESPECT and HONOR for The Master he makes every effort to walk so close to everyday. Can Brian miss it? Of course he can, he's human like the rest of us.

But when the heat's on and the battle is raging, this is a man of God you want praying in your corner."

Bless you my Brother!
You have impacted my life and ministry profoundly.
Aaron Jones
Minister, Artist and Publisher
Tulsa, Oklahoma

Author's Preface

As I sit down to write this book directed by the Holy Spirit, my heart crys out with all the pain that our Father has for His children. I didn't understand how the Lord saw His bride until the Lord took me to the books of Lamentations and Haggai. What the Lord has told me to share are very hard words for The Church; His bride. If you really have a love for our Lord, ask Him to reveal everything He must say to His people. Then write me and the Lord willing, we will meet: first to agree in spirit, then in truth, maybe even meet in person - that would truly bless me.

The Lord loves us so much, but we so easily forget His devotion to us, and then get caught up in serving self rather than serving Him.

Some might consider me a religious man, but religion and ritual bring nothing but bondage. How can I say that?

Were not the Pharisees and Sadducees religious people? But they had no heart for God's truth: which is His Son, Jesus Christ. For if they did have a heart for God, they would not have crucified the Lord of Glory! These men were more interested in tradition and ritual than establishing a relationship. They refused to accept Jesus as their Messiah. The Bible says they were envious and jealous because of all the people that were drawn to Him by the words He spoke.

So when people try to label me religious, I ask them, "Do I speak and act like I want Jesus dead?" Of course they will answer, "No."

Then I tell them, "Then I can't be religious." This stumps them, they don't know what to label me as. That's because they don't understand it's a relationship. Do you?

Obedience is Not an Option

Obedience

Holy Spirit you are the revealer and speaker of truth, Guide my hand and heart for Your Glory. As I researched two words it was made clear that there was a vast difference between them, obedience and obedient. Listen carefully. *'Obedience'* said in Webster's, "The act of obeying" or should we say the process. Is this you? Why are you not stepping out? This is not the time for excuses but actions. Those old lines, "I was going to" or "I'd planned on it," aren't going to cut it, you either will plan to serve the King or you will serve yourself. The Spirit reminds me of a truth He spoke, "Obedience brings blessing, blessing brings freedom." So why do you keep fighting Him? Because you fear what you cannot see. "The unknown is always unstable ground in the natural." But isn't that what faith is all about? Trusting what He says, not what you see. But, let us dig a little deeper to find out if the next part fits you.

As we look again at the definition of obedience we focus on the word *'act'* and watch as the Holy Spirit convicts people of playing games with His Spirit. For when you break down the letters you find what God sees. Let me show you. "A" stands for Artificial, "C" stands for Commitment and "T" stands for Tactics. Now let's look into some specifics concerning these words.

First Artificial. Webster's says "made by man." I tell you man's rules and laws are keeping God's people in bondage. Too many churches are not teaching the people to love and serve with all their heart, soul and mind. Nor do I see to seek first The Kingdom, for if they did, then everything they longed for or desired in Him would be fulfilled. Even as the Scripture says in *Matthew 6:33, "But seek ye first the kingdom of God and His righteousness, and all these things shall be added unto you."* Notice it's not before or even during, but afterward, then you will walk in the peace that surpasses understanding. The Spirit quickens me to research this verse. First *'seek,'* Webster's said "to endeavor to obtain or reach." Is this you or are you happy staying in religion? We'll draw the line where you stand by looking at the definition for *'Endeavor'* Webster's said "a conscientious or concerted effort toward a given end." In other words, a dogmatic determination that nothing and no one will be able to keep you from your goal. But what is the goal? You will soon see. Next we research the word *'First.'* Webster's had one definition that stood out, "Ranking above all others in importance or quality." Do you see through this that your priorities must be right? It's not about your kingdom but His. Then as I researched *'Kingdom'* Strong's Concordance said, "Foundation of power." Do you see Christ must be your foundation? There can be no other. Now receive what it said when I looked at the definition in Webster's for *"foundation,"* the basis (or truth) on which a thing (or person) stands (that's for righteousness).

The Spirit quickens me to go back to *'artificial'* where Webster's says, "feigned, pretended," He says, "Draw a line in the sand and make a decision where you stand." He says, "He's tired of the games." Our confirmation comes when we research *'feign'* in Webster's where it says, "to represent falsely." I tell you it's time we show what true Christianity is all

2

about, because too many Christians have lost their witness by their actions and attitude. Do you forget the Scripture, *"If not by the grace of God there go I?"* What about the one that says, *"Think not higher of thyself than thou aught."* Do you so quickly forget we're to walk in humbleness and kindness of heart? Yes and I include myself in this as well. But we are all to strive towards that high calling in Christ Jesus. But it seems to be a battle that Satan is determined we are going to lose, by trying to fill us with bitterness and unforgiveness. I tell you he may try, but he will not win! Why? Because we are the radical remnant serving Jesus Christ! We have already been bought with a price. We are NOT our own. I am quickened to teach you about a verse we hear all the time, *"Who the son sets free is free indeed."* Holy Spirit guide me. Why doesn't the verse end with "is truly free"? Because He is talking about ownership. See Satan used to own the deed to your spirit and soul. But not anymore, now the deed has been paid in full through one drop of blood. So when Satan tries to come back and claim the property, all Jesus has to do is show His Name on the deed, signed in blood. But we must do our part in keeping the contract. How? By protecting our salvation. What I mean is not taking your new life for granted. So you are careful about what you say, what you do and where you go. I think of the verse found in *I Thessalonians 5:22, "Abstain from all appearance of evil,"* lest you cause a weak brother to stumble and fall. But there is a deeper truth He wants me to share. Turn to *Ezekiel 41:1.* We will be reading out of the New Living Translation. *"After that the man brought me into the sanctuary of the temple, he measured the wall on either side of its doorway, and they were (past tense) 10 ½ feet thick."* Now Verse 2, *"The doorway was 17 ½ feet wide and the walls on each side of it were 8 ¾ feet long."* I just saw something, "He measured the walls." So Jesus is looking to see how strong we still are. But what does the walls represent? <u>Salvation</u>. Then it says *the doorway was 17½ feet wide,* which represents <u>Revelation</u>. Now let's continue, *The walls on each side of it were 8 ¾ feet long.* This is referring to the walls of prayer and intercession. But how does this fit into the picture? I will show you by the Holy Spirit. The Lord said, *"If you take your salvation for granted, you no longer care about protecting you contract with Him."* Because every time you sin on purpose, or should we say because of your rebellion, you allow your walls to deteriorate. When this happens, the strength that is needed to support the door is lost and as a result hindrance comes in; meaning the door no longer stand firm and strong. Do you understand what I am saying? When you protect you walls of salvation, there will be no hindrance to walk through the door of revelation. Then the intercessors can ask the Father to give you wisdom, understanding and direction. All because you honor Him by protecting your salvation. Do you see it? I am reminded of the Scripture, *"He withholds no good thing to him that walks uprightly."* So protect your salvation and walk in freedom. Do you see how if you will stay in that place of surrender it will be easy to hear His Spirit speaking to you? That is what we should all want, to hear His Voice clearly. So if you long to do His will, you are already showing that you're remnant. Now study *Haggai Chapter 1* and the first part of *Chapter 2:1-3* and you will see where the prophet talks about the remnant and the residue. But know this, too many translations call it 'remnant and remnant' instead of 'remnant and residue' which reveals the truth is lost in those translations. So find a translation like the King James and do your own research and find the truth. Now, let's return to the second word under A.C.T. *'Commitment'* or commit as Webster's says, "To place in trust or charge, consign entrust." But; what are they being trusted with? Responsibility, something they don't care about and accountability, something they don't want. They will commit to working on church projects, but never follow through. They will promise to pray about needs, but no intentions of doing so. The Church will call for intercessory prayer warriors to meet Friday night at 7:00pm, and asks; "Who will be there?" You raise your hand, but never show up. Why even bother to call yourself a Christian if you're not going to walk it out? I had to tell a man who was ordained to set aside his ordination. Why? Because he didn't walk as a minister. His words were not gentle, compassionate or even sensitive, but arrogant and rude. I tell you there must be surrender and brokenness to serve Him. I am reminded of the verse, *"Many are called but few are chosen."* Why? Too many won't pay the price. For you must be prepared to be lied about, spit on, cussed out, threatened, betrayed and used, just for starters. I tell you walking as a true minister can be one of the most hellish jobs for those who want to serve the King. But wait, there is a powerful blessing for walking in this obedience. Look at *Deuteronomy 28:1-2, "And it shall come to pass if thou shalt hearken unto the voice of the Lord thy God to observe and to do all his commandments which I command thee this day, that the Lord thy God will set thee on high above all nations of the Earth."* Now *verse 2, "And all these blessings shall come on thee and overtake thee if* (meaning you must do your part) *thou shalt hearken unto the voice* (this is the key) *of the Lord thy God."* Do you understand you must hear the voice of the Holy Spirit and be willing to follow without question? So the blessing is contingent on your obedience to His Spirit. Now the last word under A.C.T. is *'Tactics.'* The word *'strategies'* comes to mind and when this is studied, we find two words that stand out "Compare Tactics." Do you see these residue people are not looking to the Holy Spirit for direction? Much less asking for His help and guidance. It's simply seeing which way looks best to fool ministers and leaders. You want the praise of man but without producing the effort that is needed to achieve it. But what's the quickest way to recognize residue, especially in the Church? Watch how many get up and leave when an altar call is given to seal the words in their heart that were spoken that day by the Spirit. So only when the residue repent do you ask them for help. And I don't mean just one time coming to the altar, it's when you see a lifestyle change. Not through words, but through a heart that shows surrender to His will and His way. In other words, brokenness must be evident in their lives. Because brokenness breaks the barrier between you and Him. So are you serious about serving the Savior? Let's find out.

Turn to *Romans 1:5, "By whom we have received grace and apostleship for obedience to the faith among all nations for His name."* Now we will break down the verse for you. First, we look at the word, *'Grace.'* The first thought that comes to my spirit is, "Divine Favor." But that is not all, for when you separate the letters it says, "God Receiving At Christ's Expense." So you can only receive grace through Christ, in other words through His love. Now, let's look at the word *'Apostleship.'* First, we will look at the word *'apostle'* in Strong's that said, "A delegate, an ambassador of The Gospel; officially a commissioner of Christ." Then when we look at the word *'commission'* in Webster's we find great re-

6

sponsibility given. Because it said, "Granting certain powers." Do you see it's in reference to healing, deliverance and impartation of gifts by the Spirit? But that's not all, it also says, "An entrusting." And when this was researched were given the word '*entrust*' which said, "To give over to another for care, protection or performance." So the Lord is directing people to you that they would receive His love and care. That responsibility my friends is only going to be put into the hands of the remnant people, why? They don't have to be told, "Minister to my hurting sheep." Now let's look at *Haggai 1:14, "And the Lord stirred up the spirit of Zerubbabel son of Shealtiel, governor of Judah, and the spirit of Joshua the son of Joseah, the high priest, and the spirit of all the remnant of the people, and they came and did work in the house of the Lord of hosts their God!"* Do you see they didn't have to be enticed or even coaxed into the work? They did it willingly because they have His heart inside them. Now, let's look at the next word in *Romans 1:5, 'Obedience,'* we have already researched this in Webster's, but wait, listen to what it said in Strong's - "Attentive hearkening, compliance or submission." My spirit was drawn to the first two words, "attentive hearkening." Now listen to what Webster's said concerning '*hearkening*' "To listen attentively." Do you see it sounds like redundant wording? So why did the Spirit draw me to this? The answer is given when we look in Strong's under the word, '*Hearkening*.' Listen to the words that came up, "To hear intelligently, gather together, carefully, certainly, consent, consider, be content, declare diligently, discern, give ear, perceive, proclaim, publish, regard, report, understand and witness." I will cover those the Holy Spirit directs me to cover. "Gather Together" Do you see you are to bring His people the remnant together to encourage and challenge each other? Along with praying with power and authority that mountains would crumble because of the agreement in spirit, but also for accountability that they would keep growing. Then, "Be content," Webster's said, "Not desiring more than what one has; satisfied." I think of the verse, *"Whatever state I am in therewith to be content."* But you will only be satisfied when you have His peace inside you. Next we look at the words "declare diligently." Listen to what Webster's says about *'declare.'* "To state with emphasis or authority and to make a declaration." But that's not all, it also says, "To proclaim one's choice." I saw two things as I wrote this, first to declare that Jesus Christ is Lord, and secondly to let the world know you have chosen to follow Jesus. To let people see He is real and alive.

I tell you the remnant will not be silent, they will shout the truth. Now, let's look at the second part of this word *'diligently.'* It is much more than what you might think, because Webster's said, "Done with persevering, painstaking effort." But this doesn't show the true level of commitment until we look at the word *'Persevere.'* Catch this, "To persist in or remain constant," meaning not waivering, no indecision and steadfast to a purpose, idea or task in the face of obstacles or discouragement. I tell you that shows determination to fight to the finish and that's what remnant are all about, they will not quit halfway to the goal. What I picture is a football player running toward the goal with ball in hand. Then all of a sudden stops and says to himself: It's too hard to keep running, because my back hurts and my knees hurt and I'm frozen. How foolish would that look to people watching you? But that's exactly what the residue people do, they think it is too hard, so they just quit. Now we look at the last part in Romans, *"For obedience to the faith among all nations for His name."* Which means you are obedient to The Word by taking The Gospel to every tribe and people, that they might know the truth and be saved from eternal damnation. Now let's look at another verse, *Romans 5:19,* *"For as by one man's disobedience many were made sinners, so by the obedience of one shall many be made righteous."* The last part of the verse is the key, do you see it? Your obedience to the Holy Spirit will allow many to come into His Kingdom. Now let's look at *Romans 6:16, "Know ye not that to whom ye yield yourself servants to obey, his servants ye are to whom ye obey."* Do you see that you show the world everyday Who you serve? How you say? By the words you speak and your actions. So ask the Holy Spirit to check your mouth everyday. What do I mean? If you start to speak and you know the words would not be pleasing to God, you must allow the Holy Spirit to stop you. Because the more your words glorify the flesh the more they are displeasing to the Father. I'm reminded of the Scripture, *"He watches over His word to perform it."* Understand there's two groups listening: the demons and the angels. So who do you want responding when you are speaking? That should be a no brainer. Never speak words that the darkness can use against you. Even today I saw evidence through a man that was trained to say what the world says, rather than what the Word does. Because he started declaring that he didn't remember as well as before. But did you hear me be in agreement with that? Hell no! Fact is I reminded him of *Proverbs 10:7* where it says, *"The memory of the just is blessed."* I said stop and think for a minute every time you say, "Before I forget" you are already declaring you won't have a good memory. I said change your words to, "While I'm thinking about it." Do you see your closing one door and opening another? This is the way it should be. Now before we move on, the Spirit impressed me to look at the word *'Yield'* in verse 16. Webster's said this, "To give up, surrender, submit." I see a couple things here, you are to give up your way for His and surrender to the cross and submit to His authority not man's. But that is not all, it also said, "To give way to that which is stonger or better." So obedient people know who to submit to. Now we look at verse 19 of the same chapter, the last part of the verse, *"Yield your members servants to righteousness unto holiness."* So an obedient person knows what it means to crucify the flesh for His Glory. "Because when the flesh is crucified, the Spirit will be glorified." Do you see the remnant has separated themselves from hearers only? The remnant have set themselves apart for His purpose and you will not be able to deter them from The Kingdom work. Meaning you won't discourage or put them in fear or even doubt, because they know who they are in Him. Watch out Satan we are getting ready to give you some black eyes because you have beat up on us long enough. Then as we look at the next verse, it must be obvious to all men that you have no will but His and that anyone that meets you will not be able to deny that you sold out to serving Him. For it says in *Romans 16:19, "For your obedience is come abroad unto all men."* So the remnant are not afraid to be different and stand for righteousness. Now as we continue our research, we find a different reference number for the verse in *1 Corinthians 14:34.* So you are already being shown this is a different type of obedience. Which is confirmed by Strong's that said, "To arrange in an orderly manner, i.e. (that is) assign or dispose to a certain position or lot." Also addict, appoint, determine, ordain and set. We need to stop for a minute and give you revelation about three words. Guide me Holy Spirit. If you're an addict, something has you hooked to a lifestyle. Being that of alcohol, drugs, pills, cigarettes or pornography. But that's not what this is in reference to, it's talking about being addicted to Christ. For you must have more of His love, His mercy, His grace and His presence in your life. More of His promises to you being fulfilled. More direction being given and confirmed through other servants. Even to remind you that there is purpose, meaning and reason to keep moving forward. No longer walking lost through life, you now have a special appointment to meet with Him, before starting your day. I call it getting your orders from headquarters before heading into the fields (or world). Even reminding you to keep your full armor on. Let me explain. You are not supposed to take it off once it's put on, but simply thanking Him that you are grateful for the armor of Christ. That you are constantly wearing *the helmet of Salvation* that protects your mind. Your *breastplate of righteousness* that covers the heart. Your *belt of truth* that holds everything in place. That *shield of faith* that gives you strength to stand on God's promises. Even when the enemy throws spears of accusation, doubt, fear, depression, condemnation and lies at you, know your faith will stand like a tall solid oak tree that is unmovable. Then the most important piece, your *sword of the Spirit* which is The Word of God that proclaims boldly to Satan, "I am a child of God, all authority has been given to me. Therefore I now use The Word of God to defeat you at every turn." When I speak with confidence such things as, "It is written rendering you powerless to stop me. For I released the angels when I spoke The Word of God." Then lastly but not of less importance, *your feet shod or covered with the gospel of peace.* I tell you Satan hates peace. Just look at all the war going on and you will understand. I'm reminded of the verse, *"Let the peace of God that surpasses all understanding guard your heart and mind through Christ Jesus."* See peace says: My faith is in place and my trust in Him secure. Then as we look at the next word *'determine,'* we've made the decision to serve Him. I just saw the word *'deter'* that I spoke of earlier, so we will not forget where our focus is supposed to be, nor the purpose for which we are called. Now let's get back to *1 Corinthians 14:14*, but before I write it, know that I struggled with this verse, because I believe women are supposed to be seen and heard. So pray for me as I search for the real truth in this verse. The verse reads, *"Let your women keep silence in the churches for it is not permitted unto them to speak, but they are commanded to be under obedience as also sayeth the law."* Holy Spirit I ask for Your guidance in revealing the truth. (Approximately 2 days later) Praise the Lord! He just gave it to me! One translation could of written it this way, *"Now concerning your law pertaining to women staying silent in the churches, this is not God's law but man's."* How do I know? Because God sees neither male nor female but spirit. Also it says *'but'* which means hold on to running with the first part of the verse. Because if the verses were in agreement the word "since" should have been used instead. So was it a mistake in the Bible? Not hardly. It was to reveal there was two laws in operation. I will show you by paraphrasing this verse,

"You say that women are to be quiet, but I tell you women are to be heard when it is directed by the Holy Spirit." Thank you Lord for the revelation. So remnant people aren't afraid to stand up and say, "Man's law is in operation not God's." I tell you it's time for the captives to be set free.

Now let's look at *2 Corinthians 7:15, "And His inward affection is more abundant toward you whilst he remembereth the obedience of you all, how with fear and trembling ye received Him."* As I read this, I see His love even increases as He remembers our obedience, reverential fear and honoring of Him. So for the remnant, we consider it an honor to serve Him. Next we look at *2 Corinthians 10:5, "Casting down imaginations and every high thing that exalteth itself against the knowledge of God, and bringing into captivity every thought to the obedience of Christ."* After study and research of this verse, it became clear this was pertaining to two different areas, one was doctrine, the other was decision. We'll look at four words to confirm it. Casting, imaginations, high and exalteth. *'Casting'* Strong's said, "Demolish and Destroy." But what are we to destroy? Imaginations or reasonings. In other words: the mental process of one who draws conclusions from observation, facts or hypotheses." That is paraphrased from Webster's. Now as we look at the word *'High'* we are not to be showing pride, arrogance or disdain, which means you are not to treat this with haughtiness, contempt or despisement. Now I hear you asking, "But what is it we are not to treat this way?" You will soon see after we look at the last word, *'Exalteth.'* This had many words in Strong's, but only one truth stood out by the Spirit, "Make to doubt." Now, receive the revelation of this. You are to demolish every understanding taught by man that

13

says, "Tongues aren't for today, healing isn't for today, deliverance is not needed today, prophecy isn't for today. All those died with the Old Testament Church." So churches keep people in bondage by making them doubt and ask: Is God really reachable? Is He really the same way He was then? Would He heal me or do I just have to suffer for Christ? Is tongues really of the devil, or is it of God? Now let's look at the second part of verse 5, *"Bringing into captivity every thought to the obedience of Christ."* Holy Spirit help me to continue to flow. But who is keeping you captive? None other than man himself. We receive confirmation of this truth when we study the word *'Captive'* in Webster's that said *'Enslaved.'* Then when we look at the word *'Enslave'* the truth gets stronger. For it said, "Reduced to slavery" (that's spiritual slavery) Then it said "Bondage" (that is bondage to man) and then it said, "Dependence." For, this word we find four definitions, but only one resonated in my spirit, "Influenced or controlled by something else," or should we say someone else other than the Holy Spirit. So obedient people are not going to give in or follow a man-pleasing spirit, but His Spirit only. Next we look at Philemon verse 21, *"Having confidence in thy obedience I wrote thee, knowing that thou wilt do more than I say."* Then as I was researching *'Confidence'* in Strong's, these words stood out, "agree, assure, believe, obey, persuade, trust and yield." Now Holy Spirit help me to brake these down. You agree and do what needs to be done, you are assured with confidence that you have heard from Him, you believe in your heart that you are following the Spirit, you obey because there is no other way. You are not persuaded by man to change directions, you trust what He's doing in and through you and you yield to His Spirit with total and complete surrender. Next we look at *Hebrews 5:8, "Though he were a son, yet learned obedience by the things which he suffered."* Now I will write it a different way. Though you are a child of God you still learn obedience by the things you suffer for His Name. Understand you are going to suffer physically then have to endure ridicule, mockery, emotional stress and slander, just for standing in righteousness. But this truth is no surprise to the remnant, fact is they could probably write a book about pain, I know I could. But the more pain I endure, the greater the glory of Him revealed. Let's look at some Scriptures. First *Romans 8:18, "For I reckon that the sufferings of the present time are not worthy to be compared with the glory which shall be revealed <u>in us</u>."* So right there you see confirmation. Now we will look at two more Scriptures and see if you can pick out the common denominator in all three. So turn to *1 Peter 1:11, "Searching what or what manner of time the Spirit of Christ which was in them did signify, when it testified beforehand the sufferings of Christ, and the Glory that should follow."* This is one of those verses that you don't know what it is in reference to until research is done. So let's look at the words "Searching, manner, time, signify, testified, beforehand and suffering." As I studied, *'searching,'* these words stood out in Strong's, "Speak, command and preach". Do you see we are supposed to speak the word and take command or our authority over darkness and preach deliverance to the captives? Then as we look at the word, *'Manner'* we see what should be our concern. We start with *'Bear'* or bare one another's burdens, then "Bring Forth", that's life and revelation then *'Endure'* that's hardships like any good soldier would. Then "Reach" that's out to the lost and hurting. Now as we look at the word 'Time' we see this is the "Season" to start gathering the harvest. Then we use every "Occasion" just like Paul did to witness to people and then know this is the "Messianic Period" or biblical time because prophecies are coming to pass, fast. The Holy Spirit reminds me of a truth He spoke to me fairly recently, "It's time for the book of Daniel to come to pass." Because the "many days are here" *(cf. Daniel 8:26)*. Now we continue with "Signify" that said three things, "To make plain" meaning you must be born again and accept Christ and that there is no eternal life without Him. Now I need to make one thing clear, you will either have an eternity with Him or Satan. Because you will not be able to escape judgement. Then "signify" said "Declare," meaning speak with authority they are healed and that judgement is coming to the wicked. Then, "Shew," show forth His mighty works as a servant of God. Then when we look at the word 'Testified' we see three words stand out, "Predict, Adduced and Obtest." As we look at 'Predict' we find what the remnant willingly do "make known in advance," meaning tell or warn. It also said, "Especially on the basis of special knowledge" or *words of knowledge* given by the Holy Spirit. So here you see the remnant are all about saving lives and winning souls for Him. Then we study two words that some would not be familiar with, but hold on, there's revelation in them. Because when "Adduced is researched in Webster's we find we're "to cite as an example" or "call them to a place of action." Meaning not sitting in the pews, but out on the front lines, laying their life down for His. Next we look at the word, 'Obtest' Webster's said "Protest." The first thing I think of is support rallies, such as Pro-Life demonstrations showing you stand for life and righteousness. But that's not all, it also said, "Supplicate and Entreat." Webster's said this about "Supplicate," "To ask for humbly or earnestly as by praying". I think of standing in the gap or intercession. That's not just for people, but a nation as well. Now let's look at *'Entreat,'* Webster's said, "Plead with." I think of crying out for mercy for those who are lost. Do you see the remnant are all about Kingdom work? Now let's look at *'Beforehand'* in *1 Peter 1:11*. Webster's had this definition which stood out by the Spirit, "In advance." So here you see you're supposed to warn or prophesy in advance as any Prophet or Seer would do. But what is a *see-er*? They are a gifted person that's been allowed to actually see destruction coming, be it in the natural realm wreaking havoc, or spiritual realm trying to bring destruction, chaos and possibly even death.

Now let's look at the last word in *1 Peter 1:11*, "Sufferings." There are two things I am supposed to show you, the first you already know, you will have to endure, "Hardship or Pain" for the Gospel's sake. But wait, did you know it also said, "Proper suffering"? Which is what? "Paying the price" so that new strength, new anointing, new depth would come to your spirit. Then through your suffering people would see the hand of God and Christ as a result of it. Now let's look at some Scriptures for more understanding, starting with *Philippians 3:10*. Holy Spirit help me as I continue. When I read this verse, I saw three things for the first time. We start with, *"That I may know Him,"* that is for both the seasoned Christian to learn new depths of His love and the new believer learning about His love. Because some wonder if God is real or just a religious crutch. Then the second thing I saw was, *"The power of His resurrection,"* in other words changing you, bringing you from fleshly life to a spiritual one. Giving you life and not what you have been deceived in believing was life. And lastly, *"The fellowship of His suffering."* I tell you now it is much more than what you might of thought. Follow with me as we research *'Fellowship'* and learn what it is to walk with Him.

First I will give you the words the Holy Spirit directed me to, then give you understanding of each. Strong's said, "Sharer, Companion, Resemblance and Denoting Union." So we are to be a sharer of His pain and a companion by choice, choosing to follow Him. Then we start to resemble Him, meaning beginning to look like Him in spirit, with mercy and grace flowing through us and forgiveness operating within. Now "Denoting Union," for this understanding we look to Webster's which said, "Serve as a symbol of relationship." So it shows people Who you're leaning on and trusting in. Are you ready for more? Then turn to *Acts 5:40-41, "When they had called the apostles and beaten them."* The Spirit stops me to say, if you are called as an Apostle, know that Satan will beat you up anyway he can, meaning physically, spiritually, mentally, emotionally and financially. Anything to stop you from establishing churches of righteousness. I tell you that needed to be heard myself. Now the next part of this verse, *"They commanded that they should not speak in the name of Jesus."* The first thing that comes to mind is schools not being allowed to mention God, much less His Son Jesus. But you must recognize man being used by darkness to shut you up. Even to get you to justify compromise, so you don't offend anyone. But remnant are not interested in man's approval, but God's. I tell you remnant will not be silenced. Continuing with *verse 41, "and they departed from the presence of the council.*" See, man will try to show you what's necessary and acceptable, Why? So everyone stays happy. Heaven forbid if we were to convict anybody of sin. Also, wrong counsel will put you in bondage, but the right counsel will set you free. Understand you must recognize counsel given by the flesh from that given by the Spirit. Because one will keep you safe, the other will bring destruction. Now the last part of verse 41, *"Rejoicing that they were counted worthy to suffer shame for His name."* Wait a minute, *"Worthy to suffer shame?"* Yes this is part of "Proper Suffering." I think of the Scripture, *"For thy sake I have borne reproach."* That's *Psalm 69:7.*

The Spirit impressed me to research, "Borne and Reproach." *'Borne'* in the Strong's said, "accept, suffer, bear, forgive, give, help, hold up, lay, magnify, respect, spare and yield." Now the Spirit will break it down: You are to accept this is the price for walking with Him; to suffer in the flesh for His glory; then bear one another's burdens; forgive those who have lied about you; give your finances by the direction of the Holy Spirit; help those in need and hold up in prayer those who need direction or breakthrough. Then willing to lay down your life and humble yourself: never thinking higher of yourself than you ought. Then allow Him to magnify Himself through you. Respect the opinions of others, remembering they're spiritual babies, then learn to listen and spare your words of criticism and lastly, yielding to the Holy Spirit through love and respect. Now let's look at the words under *'reproach.'* Strong's said, "Contumely, Disgrace, Rebuke, Shame, Defame, Blaspheme, Defy, Jeopard and Upbraid." First let's look at *'Contumely'* in Webster's to see what it means. I tell you one word hits a lot of areas. Listen: "Rudeness, contempt in behavior or speech, and insolence, meaning; presumptuous, insulting and arrogant." All this for following Jesus? Yes, so the public and the religious want to make a mockery of us, rebuke us for any number of things, speaking in tongues, words of knowledge, telling us when a truth is spoken by the Spirit, "That's a matter of interpretation." No it isn't, not when it's <u>done by the Spirit!</u> Then try to shame by putting a false guilt on us, then they are out to defame you by attacking your good name by slander or libel. Are you getting the picture of how much we have to endure? Then blaspheme, meaning you might as well get used to the fact people will curse you because of what you stand for. Now we look at the word "defy" and find there will be many that challenge you in your beliefs. I told someone recently, "It doesn't matter what you believe as long as it lines up with the Word of God." That's a truth people don't want to hear. Then there are those who will put your life in jeopardy or peril. I just saw someone pushing you in front of an oncoming bus. This is the kind of hellish things Satan will do when you come against his kingdom. *"Father concerning this person, I cancel Satan's assignment right now and I plead the blood of Jesus over them and a ring of blood around them."* Now, before I go any further, I'm supposed to show you a powerful Scripture for protection. So turn to *1 Peter 5:5*, the middle part of the verse, *"Yea all of you be subject one to another and be clothed with humility."* But you may say, "How does this verse protect me?" I'll explain this as the Holy Spirit unveils it. About 5 years ago, the Holy Spirit began teaching me a warfare prayer that's now done everyday right after midnight. So listen and receive,

"I bind the principalities and the powers of darkness

and the rulers of darkness in high places this day in Je-sus' Name and I pray confusion in the enemy's ranks this day in Jesus' Name. Then I blind the eyes of the en-emy and deafen their ears, all this day in Jesus' Name."

But even after doing all that, it wasn't stopping cars from crossing the double yellow line, trying to hit me. So I cried out to the Lord in frustration, "How come if I have blinded the eyes of the enemy he can see me?" Now receive what the Lord spoke. "The darkness doesn't see you, it's attacking the glory." He said, "It's like a Pac-Man game, when the energy chip is eaten, he starts flashing to take out the enemy." He said, "You are like a beacon flashing with my Glory." Then I asked, "How do I keep the darkness from seeing the Glo-ry?" That's when He directed me to *1 Peter 5:5*. He said, "If you will ask me to cover you with a cloak of humility, the darkness can't see the Glory." He said, "You'll become like a Stealth Bomber in the spirit realm. You'll move with speed, silence and power under the radar of the enemy." Now I must warn you about something, since the darkness no lon-ger knows where you are at, it will have people call you, try-ing to find your location. Saying something like, "Hi Susan, where are you at right now?" I tell you, DON'T give them a hint, just say I am out taking care of business; What do you need? Now receive this truth and walk in supernatural pro-tection. Now, let's look at the last word under "Reproach," "Upbraid," Webster's said, "To reprove sharply." So these kind of people will search to find fault in your teaching or even your character, and cut you with their words if pos-sible. But that's not all, it also said, "To scold or chide ve-hemently." Meaning they are stating disapproval violently.

But will any of these things stop the remnant? No. Matter of fact it makes them more determined to keep going. Now we'll research one more Scripture under "Obedience," *1 Peter 1:2, "Elect according to the foreknowledge of God the Father, through sanctification of the Spirit unto obedience and sprinkling of the blood of Jesus Christ. Grace unto you and peace be multiplied."* Again, here we see a Scripture people read with no understanding, that is until now. So by the Holy Spirit let's all receive hidden truth, revelation and life. We start with researching six words, "Elect, Foreknowledge, Sanctification, Sprinkling, Grace and Multiplied." As I studied "Elect" or should we say remnant, we see not what a life should be about, but what it already is. Because we have made the <u>choice</u> to follow Him and not the world. We <u>lay</u> our life before Him to use us as He pleases. We break the code of <u>silence</u> and speak openly about the truth of Christ, declaring boldly The Word because we don't fear their faces. We are ready to give an <u>answer</u> to those who would try to trip us up with religious questions, because we know it won't be us that speaks, but Him. We recognize when someone is spiritually exhausted and <u>bring a word</u> of encouragement. We are to <u>call</u> sin what it is and bring people to a place of repentance, call life into corpses and call for unity in the body of Christ and put an end to this 'he said, she said' nonsense. Because it does nothing but glorify man. Then affirm brothers and sisters in Christ that their walk is pleasing to the Lord. Then <u>preach</u> the Good News Message. I just saw something in "preach," take the "P" away and it is "Reach." So for some it takes preaching to reach the lost. But not always with your mouth, you can preach a message about who you serve just by your walk. I heard someone say, "I'd rather see a semon than hear one." Now listen to this last statement for "Elect." <u>"To shine or make manifest by rays."</u> Do you see that's the glory they cannot deny you shine with? Do you see how serious the "Elect" are? That is how we should all be. Now let us look at *'Foreknowledge.'* The first thing I see is being made aware of what the enemy is up to by the Holy Spirit. Let me explain. When you start praying in tongues by the leading of the Spirit, then the Holy Spirit has feedom to visit the enemy's camp, listen to their plans, then come back and inform you of tricks and traps designed to discourage, derail or destroy you. For this confirmation turn to *2 Kings 6:8*, we will be looking at the New Living Translation for this one. *"When the King of Aram was at war with Israel he would confer with his officers and say, "We will mobilize our forces at such and such a place."* Now verse 9, *"But immediately Elisha the man of God would warn the king of Israel, "do not go near that place for the Aramean's are planning to mobilize their troops there."* So here you see a leader gives warning and guidance by the Spirit to keep all alive. But why was Elisha able to hear so clearly? Two words, *'Surrender'* and *'Submission'* with a servant's heart. Because a true servant always knows what the will of the Master is. Now watch and see how this frustrates the enemy, verse 11, *"The King of Aram became very upset over this. He called his officers together and demanded, "Which of you is the traitor? Who has been informing the King of Israel of my plans?"* Now listen to what is known and spoken in verse 12, *"It is not us my lord the king, one of the officers replied, Elisha the prophet in Israel tells the King of Israel even the words you speak in the privacy of your bedroom."* Isn't it interesting the darkness is well aware where the power is and who is walking in it? Surrender is the key to praying out the mysteries or should we say secrets of The Kingdom, that we might receive direction and protection. Now we continue with "Foreknowledge" and study three words, "Perceive, Resolved and Be Sure." As we research "Perceive" in Strong's we find it has several reference numbers, so it shows there is much truth to be revealed.

Now Holy Spirit help me as I break these down. First we are to "be aware" of our surroundings and to "consider" what is before us. Is it a stepping stone or a stumbling block? Then we are to "have knowledge" about what is before us. Is it deception trying to fool us or direction being given by His Spirit? Because if we are in tune with Him, we will be able to "discern clearly." No confusion only clarity. So when the enemy tries "to rush upon" you, he is taken out by a surprise attack from a place he wasn't expecting. Then when you are in a religious church that would try "to toss" you about with *every wind of doctrine*, you won't be moved to the intellectual realm, but steadfast in the spiritual one. You won't be "sore troubled" because the Spirit has already showed you what's coming and how to prepare for it. You are "obstinate" about your stand, meaning you adhere to an attitude, opinion or course of action given by the Spirit. We are "fiercely" loyal to our King and Lord. We will "declare" to the world they must be saved and "show" them the way of salvation. We stand watch as a "sentry" or guard to make sure no wolves in sheep's clothing sneak in. Then we know what it means to be "clothed" in humility and covered with His "raiment" of righteousness. We recognize and "seize" opportunities to witness to the religious or lost. We are not afraid when "opposition" arises for we know it is nothing more than confirmation that we

24

are going the right direction. Then we "accept" this is the price one must pay to follow Him, and then "receive" our reward for obedience. Now let's look at the last two words, "Resolved" and "Be sure." Resolved said, "Fixed in purpose, resolute." Then "Resolute" said, "Pursuing a fixed purpose, unwavering." Understand you must know your purpose once you accept Christ and surrender to serve Him. Because now everything you have or that's been given to you, is to be used for His Glory. Why do you think He gave you such a large house? Certainly not just to dust! Why do you have five cars, to drive a different one each day of the week? Not hardly! It is to help people in need. Like when a missionary comes home and struggles just to get from place to place because they don't have transportation. These people are on the front lines so they should receive the best when they come home for a rest and gather new financial supporters. They should be booked up to speak in churches with hearts that are ready to help. Not frustrated because no one wants to hear the burden the Lord has put in their heart. Now we look at "Be sure," Webster's said, "Incapable of being doubted or disputed," "Not hesitating or wavering; stable and steady, firm and confident of some future possibility. So the elect or remnant don't have to question if they heard from the Spirit, they will move forward with absolute confidence. I think of the Scripture, *"My sheep know my voice and the voice of another they will not follow."* Now let's study 'Sanctification,' but before we do, the Spirit quickens me to share a truth that came one day as I was teaching about remnant. He said, "There's remnant that don't know they're remnant, ...they aren't even saved yet." It's as if they can see the vanity of pursuing the world and everything in it. So ask God to show you where the hidden remnant are, because He says, "They are ready to receive me." I tell you it's time for the Radical Remnant to ARISE! Now get bold and show people the futility in following religion! I pray you are getting stirred up as I write, for this book is a call to arms in the Spirit realm for the remnant. But what is remnant? We get our answer from Webster's that said, "A small remaining group of people." Remaining? - in what way? Our answer comes when we research, 'sanctification' in Strong's and come up with several words, but only these stood out: "Purification, Holiness, Consecrate, Blameless, Clean, Innocent, Modest and Chaste." So the remnant cry out to be taken through the purifying process, then they don't walk in holiness, but live in it. They've made the decision to consecrate their life, meaning set themselves apart for His glory. They are blameless, meaning they don't point the finger at someone else for their own shortcomings; they are not afraid to take accountability for their actions, because they listen and follow the spirit. Then they are clean, meaning they refuse to defile their body. Also their ways are sacrificial, not self-serving: not manipulating to get, but surrendered to give. They're also innocent of wrong doings, because they can't be bought by the darkness. We receive our confirmation when we look up 'Innocent' in Webster's that says, "Uncorrupted by evil." Then they are modest in clothing, meaning things aren't worn to cause any stumbling in the body of Christ. They are also not "pretentious," What do I mean? They are not about position or status. Again we receive confirmation through Webster's that says, "Claiming or demanding a position of distinction or merit; especially when unjustified." So remnant are not about titles: but tenure. Meaning they are more interested in permanent placement in Him, because of endurance through time. Understand promotion comes from Him, when you have been found faithful. But that's not all, it also comes through quietness with trust. Even as I'm reminded of a truth the Holy Spirit spoke one day, "When you're more interested in listening then speaking, God has promotion in mind." But why? Because He knows when you open your mouth, it won't be about exalting self, but Him. Holy Spirit help us to remember this truth, Amen.

Now we have one word left under sanctification, "Chaste." I tell you this is a subject many churches will not address, because they themselves are not about purity, but intellectual performance. <u>Impressing you with their words, not their walk.</u> Whereas the remnant are all about being "morally pure" as Webster's said. So they are all about teaching truth by the Spirit, not by the flesh and imparting noble character. I pray you are being challenged and encouraged as you receive these truths and recognizing you're remnant as a result. Now, let's look at the three words left under *1 Peter 1:2,* "Sprinkling, Grace and Multiplied." Sprinkling may surprise you, because if you were raised Catholic like I was, your first thought would have been baptism right? Where you were sprinkled over a fountain as a ritual, but no impartation. Which just shows it is a man-made thing. Then when I looked up *'Sprinkling'* in Strong's it gave one word that opened the door for revelation "Aspersion" and when this was researched we find three definitions for it. First, the traditional one some would already know, but wait, listen to this second one, "a calumnious report or remark, slander." Let's touch on "Slander," Webster's said, "Injurious to the reputation or wellbeing of a person." But what about "Calumnious," what's the truth here? Again Webster's comes to our aid when we look up the word, 'Caluminate' that says, "To make false statements." So if it's "Calum<u>nious</u>" it's a continuation of defilement of reputation and character. Do you see how strong the remnant must be? We will not compromise! Truly obedience is not an option for us. Now let's move to "Grace." For this word I start with a question I asked the Holy Spirit one day; "What do the letters of "grace" stand for?" He said, "God Receiving at Christ's Expense." Yet there are many who have taken that Grace for granted, forgetting about the price that was paid for their salvation. Now receive what Strong's said about "Grace." "The divine influence upon the heart and its reflection in the life." Ponder on that. Then it said, "Acceptable, Benefit, Favor, Gift, Joy, Liberality and pleasure." Now Holy Spirit point me to the ones that need to be talked about.

First, "Benefit," I think of a dinner arranged to bring awareness to a specific need that all would be blessed as a result of giving. Like a homeless shelter receiving much needed funds to meet the basic needs of towels, washcloths and soap. But you may ask; How is that a win win situation? Because as the hopeless and homeless hear the truth about Christ and His love, they have an opportunity to be changed forever. Then those former homeless now become helpers and leaders, reaching out to a type of people they know well. Maybe even help put legislation in place to assist those who were once lost to get started again by fixing up homes that are now abandoned and eyesores to the community. Making them safe houses for women who have been abused because of drugs or alcohol, or halfway houses for people who have come out of prison. Next let's look at *'Favor'* Webster's said, "A gracious kind or friendly attitude." Do you see this is what allows His grace to move in our behalf? Not a: "you own me" attitude, but a humble and grateful one. Not walking in anything but expectancy believing to be blessed, not trying to make it happen. Like when ministers ask for a "Preacher's discount" which is straight up wrong. Let me show you how it is supposed to work through a divine appointment orchestrated by the Holy Spirit. I was on the east side of town when the Spirit spoke saying, "Go to the Taco Bell on 71st Street." So I got in my truck and headed for the west side of town. When I got there, I was then directed to go inside, so I grabbed my Word and headed for the front counter to place my order. But when I opened my mouth to speak, the Holy Spirit took over and started speaking specific words to the lady taking the order. Telling her He had heard her cry and was answering. Now I don't remember everything I said, only what He reminds me of. Now listen to her response, she said, "I just came from the bathroom and had been crying out to God." So this was confirmation that I had heard correctly. Now listen to what took place next, after placing my order. She said that the total was a dollar and some change. I first thought she just heard wrong, but then was reassured she heard correctly. She said, "I wanted to give it to you free, but had to charge you something." I tell you I was almost in tears over her kindness and generosity. Do you see this is the way it is supposed to be? This is the way remnant are, surrendered. Now let's look at *"Liberality,"* the Scripture comes to mind, *"Where the Spirit of the Lord is there's liberty and freedom."* Then when I researched *'liberty,'* these words stood out, "Not a slave, bring, fallout and light." So you are not a slave to sin

anymore and you are not ashamed to bring Him your brokenness. Then when I saw the words, "Fallout," I thought of
being slain in the Spirit, where you end up on the floor, which
is the place of submission and surrender. Apparently this
place in the Spirit is important, this is the second time it is
spoken about. Then as I saw the word *'Light,'* I was reminded
of the Scripture, *"Let your light so shine before men that they
would see that good work and glorify your father which is in
heaven."* Do you see that you are being a living testimony
through your walk? To be a living epistle for all men to read.
Now the Holy Spirit directs me to research, *'Submission'* and
'Surrender.' Webster's said this about, "Submission or submit," Surrender (oneself) to the will or authority of another."
Do you see that is the Holy Spirit? Then when I looked up
'surrender' Webster's said, "To give up or give back that which
has been granted." Which means you traded death for life
and then gave your life back to Him that He might use you for
His Glory. Now we look at the last word under *1 Peter 1:2*,
"Multiplied." I tell you it is so much more than just increase.
But let's get real; What's the first thing that comes to mind, are
you thinking in the right realm? How about increase in the
anointing to minister life unto those that are dead? I think of
the Scripture, *"Let the dead bury the dead."* Sadly I see so
many people who are spiritually dead and don't even know it.
Which shows they are just operating in religion. Even recently I was talking to a man about a remnant church the
Holy Spirit directed me to, hoping he would show interest
and ask questions as a result. But such was not the case, because he shut down instead. Why are people settling for ritual rather than relationship? Because they think they have
enough. What really makes this sad is that I have known this

man for a long time and we have even talked about Christ and the things of God. But when I encouraged him to go deeper he became offended. I tell you it's so obvious there is a need for people to be filled with the abundance of His Spirit. Because the Holy Spirit is the power that is necessary to win our battles. Actually, He is the turbo-booster in the spirit realm, a supernatural power that is available to you, if you want it. So why would you want to move at a snail's pace instead of supersonic? It is a mystery. I think of the Scripture, *"Without me you can do nothing, but with me (the Holy Spirit) you can do all things."* It is so clear we need course correction. But who will receive that truth? Only the remnant. Now let's look at the words that came up when we researched, "Multiplied," in Strong's, "Throng, Populace, Accomplish, Imbue, Influence, To Inspire, Permeate and Pervade." Holy Spirit continue to guide me. "Throng" said, "To press in upon." So we must press in to His presence and have more of Him. But it's more than that, it's laying at His feet crying out to Him until the answer comes. <u>Even fasting to show God you are serious about getting answers and receiving your breakthrough.</u> I tell you there are so many in that place, desperate for direction. But rest in the fact that He knows your heart and motives. I speak that to you, rest in the fact He knows your heart. So quit being so hard on yourself. Next let's look at "Imbue." I tell you this one I said yes to the minute I read the definition, "To make thoroughly wet, saturate." Do you see you are full of His Spirit both inside and out? So full of Him that people are convicted standing in your presence because of the anointing that operates in and through you. I tell you I am not satisfied just praying for people. I want to minister <u>healing for every area of their life.</u> Healing for cancer, healing for depression, twisted limbs, broken backs, incurable diseases, things that would cause the world to take notice. So are you ready to make a difference? If you are, then ask Him to use you. Ask Him to bring you a person that has been fighting migraines. Then when you lay hands on them they are instantly healed. But not only that, they tell you heat was felt and power flowing through them. Now I hear you saying; Who me? Yes you! Don't ever think you have to be super-spiritual to be used. That's a lie from the pits of hell. He's simply looking for willing vessels. Because there is no perfect formula for people to receive healing, just sensitive serving ones following His Spirit. Now, let's look at '*Influence*,' the definition that stood out was, "Power to sway or affect based on prestige, wealth, ability or position." <u>Question</u>: Do you have the ability to convince people there will be a price they must pay for their sin? To show them it is not about prestige, but position in Him. That the true wealth is found in His Word, not in the world. To remind them all their abilities come from Him and Him alone. Next, let's look at '*Inspire*.' Listen to the definition that stood out, "To affect or arouse by divine influence." Do you see the divine influence is the Holy Spirit? He's The One Who guides and directs; He is The One Who changes you from following religion to seeking relationship. Because religion brings death, relationship life. But, who really wants life? <u>Answer</u>: Only the remnant. Only they will do the work willingly, whereas the residue must be reminded and coaxed. Even to be shown that things are not as they once were. For confirmation turn to *Haggai 1:12, "Then Zerubbabel, the son of Shealtiel and Joshua the son of Josedech the high priest, with all the remnant of the people, obeyed the voice of the Lord their God and the words of Haggai the prophet.*" Let's look at this verse a little. The people recognized and obeyed the voice of the Spirit of God speaking through the prophet, because remnant are attentive, looking and listening to His Spirit. But more than that, they are devoted to serving the King of Kings and Lord of Lords. Now, what about the residue? They have to be woke up, that includes leaders that are no longer hearing or following the Spirit. But how do you recognize residue? Easy, they are all about serving self and they will get upset if you challenge them to seek a relationship, especially with the Holy Spirit. I confirm this through a woman I met. Let me explain, she had a situation that needed to be dealt with, so I suggested we pray and ask the Holy Spirit for guidance. Do you know the minute I introduced the Holy Spirit into the equation she got upset and said, "I don't need that!" I don't get it. Refusing to pray in agreement and ask the Holy Spirit for direction? I tell you she was offended by my suggestion. Church, do you see what's happened?

Now let's go back to Haggai and find out there's leaders who think they are remnant, when in reality they are residue. For this confirmation, look with me in *Haggai 2:2,* "*Speak now to Zerubbabel the son of Shealtiel governor of Judah and to Joshua the son of Josedech the high priest.*" Wait a minute, let's stop here. Weren't these leaders already addressed as remnant? No, look carefully, only in verse 2 of chapter 2 do you see the verse starting with, "*Speak now.*" In chapter 1 they proclaimed themselves as remnant. Do you see it? Then as we continue in chapter 2, we see it says, "*And to the residue of the people.*" That means along with those leaders. Now look what has to be spoken to the residue in verse 3 of chapter 2, "*Who is left among you that saw this house in her first glory? And how do you see it now? Is it not in your eyes in comparison of it as nothing?"* Holy Spirit help me. They have to be shown something very powerful is missing, but; What is it? The Glory, the weight of His presence. You became so carnal you weren't even looking for it any more. I tell you I've walked into churches that felt like a morgue. No life of any kind present, only death. Do you see the truth? God wants us multiplying in the right area. John said it right, *"He must increase but I must decrease." (John 3:30).* Now let's bring the truth home through researching *'Permeate.'* Webster's said, "To spread or flow throughout; pervade." Do you see we are to be spreading The Good News of Jesus Christ? But not by operating in flesh, that will never work; only by the leadings and promptings of the Spirit will people be able to receive. So you must recognize the nudging in your spirit and move on it. Now let me say this, if you are remnant, you want all people to repent and turn to Him, but only the Holy Spirit knows who's ready to receive. So don't get anxious in your pursuit of the lost, stay sensitive to His Spirit and you won't miss the mark. I tell you, He wants His Spirit flowing through you like a torrential river. Like a Power Station of His Spirit. Because greater the surrender the more His anointing can flow. Now we close "Obedience" with this truth from *Deuteronomy 28:1,* *"And it shall come to pass if thou shalt hearken diligently unto the voice* (this is the key) *of the Lord thy God to observe and to do all his commandments which I command thee this day"* now verse 2, *"All these blessings shall come on thee and overtake thee if thou shalt hearken unto the voice of the Lord thy God."* Do you see it is contingent on you doing your part? But; What is that part? You must respond to His voice.

Obedient

Now we study *'Obedient'* and see what the Holy Spirit reveals. Let's begin by looking at *Exodus 24:7, "and he took the book of the covenant and read in the audience of the people, and they said, all that the Lord hath said will we do and be obedient."* Right off the bat we see what looks like redundancy with the word "do" along with "obedient". But not so, for when we look in Strong's, the words, "call or gather together, consider and declare" stand out. So obedient or remnant know the importance of bringing the body together, challenging them to take His Word deep into their heart and speak His Word with authority. For they do not fear man's face, nor will they ever. Because they've determined to be change agents for Christ. Do you see through this verse they've already decided who they are going to serve? "I think of the verse *'choose this day who you are going to serve.'* I thank God I have already decided Who I am living for, I may cry many tears, but I will not quit. Because He is changing me from the inside out, doing a work I cannot see, but others can." Now let's look at *Numbers 27:20,* this talks about Joshua being prepared to take the place of Moses as leader. *"And thou shalt put some of thine honor upon him, that all the congregation of the children of Israel may be obedient."* The first thing we see is honoring or respecting your authority. But more than that, for when we research *'honor'* in Strong's, three words stand out, "Beauty, Comeliness and Excellency." Now watch

35

as the revelation unfolds through "Excellency" by Webster's, "A title or form of address for certain high officials, such as ambassadors, bishops or governors." Holy Spirit help me. Do you see you become officers and generals in the spirit realm? Like John G. Lake and Smith Wigglesworth. Walking with such authority that demons tremble and flee at your presence. But understand this, it comes at a price. I know, I've cried enough tears to fill an ocean. But the anointing increases with every tear. There's been times I cried so hard, I almost couldn't walk. But through it, the captives are being set free. Now let's look at another part of this verse, *"that all the congregation of the children."* Wait a minute. Why doesn't it just say, "All the children of Israel"? Because we have a hidden truth with *'Congregation.'* Listen to the words I found, "Witness, Recorder, Stand upright and Give warning." So this remnant aren't afraid to tell truth about life in Christ and having your name recorded in the Lamb's Book of Life. To show people there's things they must stand against and others they must stand for, like purity, holiness, righteousness. Honesty and integrity, just for starters. But that's not all, they will warn all those who have an ear to hear. But, what are we to warn them of? Two things: judgement and destruction for a people and nation who turn their back on God. Because, "A nation that turns its back on God is cursed." But, why did they turn away? They started listening to the voice of Satan that said, "There is no God." But what deception did he use? Evolution; a lie that says God did not create the world. Therefore there's no such thing as sin, much less payment for it. So *everyone just does what is right in their own eyes:* with no accountability. But God says, *"They will have to give an account before me."* Hear that! So cry out to Him before it's too late, because things are winding down. The evidence is all around us. Now before we move on, I am reminded again to tell you what the Lord said to me concerning the book of Daniel. He said, "The verse that speaks about, *"Shutting up the vision that shall not be till many days"* has now come to pass." He said, "The many days are here." Do you get this? This is how short time is, so study Daniel and ask the Holy Spirit to open your eyes with understanding and get the warning message out to His people. Because the destruction is imminent, meaning it's about to occur. But don't take my word alone, ask the Lord to show you and then confirm what's coming and when He does, pray, pray like never before.

Do you begin to see that obedience cannot be an option? It must be a lifestyle – one of surrender. Now let's look at *Deuteronomy 4:30, "When thou art in tribulation and all these things are come upon thee, even in the latter days, if thou turn to the Lord thy God and shalt be obedient unto his voice."* Now look what will happen because you are being obedient in verse 31, *"He will not forsake thee neither destroy thee, nor forget the covenant of thy father's which he swore unto them."* Do you see the powerful promise? Then let's do some research with "Tribulation, Latter, Forsake and Covenant." Holy Spirit guide me. When we study *'tribulation'* in Strong's, specific words stand out, "Narrow, afflicted, anguish, distress and sorrow." As we look at 'Narrow,' I think of the Scripture, *"Wide is the path of destruction and many that go therein, but narrow is the path of righteousness and few there be that find it."* Are you familiar with this verse? If not, you're about to get your eyes opened. Because I've researched this word before and it is not what you think. For it does not mean a limited ability to enter, but in truth it

37

means, through the heartache and pain you are being kept close to Him, always relying on His Spirit. Want confirmation? Then look at *Matthew 7:14* and research the word *'narrow'* in Greek. When you do, you will see Strong's says, "Afflict, suffer and trouble." Then when we look at the next word *'latter'* in Deuteronomy chapter 4 we find Strong's giving us a mix, "Last, end, hinder, remnant, residue and reward." Do you see the truth yet? We are in the last days, which is why the battle is so great. Because the darkness is determined to hinder or stop us. The Spirit impresses me to look in Webster's under *'hinder,'* "To obstruct or delay the progress of; prevent; to stop." Does that make it clear you are going the right direction? Then the remnant, not the residue will be rewarded for their faithfulness and obedience. Now the Spirit quickened me to look at this verse again and points out, *"If thou turn to the Lord."* So this shows even the rebellious can be blessed if they repent and turn from their wicked ways. But turning and being obedient are two different things. Because one just wants to escape the fire of judgement, the other is running harder towards Him. Now let's look at the next word in *Deuteronomy 4:30–31, 'Forsake.'* For this one we look to Strong's and come up with two words, "Abate and Consume." Holy Spirit guide me. When we think of forsake we think of not being abandoned right? But it doesn't mean there won't be battle, that will still happen, instead He will give you grace to go through it. We receive this confirmation when we research *'abate'* and come up with, "To reduce in amount, degree or intensity." So in His grace, the intensity of the battle is lessened, that through His strength you can go through it. I tell you I needed to hear that myself. Because I just had a hellish

mountain blow up in my face, it was so intense it left me numb. Even now I wonder - how can a God Who says He loves me so much, allow this hell to happen? Because all the signs point to the fact that this occurrence may have changed my future. Even now it is taking everything in me to keep writing. So is it easy to be obedient? NO. Especially when He gives you a Word of judgement for someone you know, who has been playing games with His Spirit. I tell you God is not mocked. Even now I am asking for confirmation of what He had me speak. Because in the mouth of 2 or 3 witnesses every word is confirmed. Now, let's look at the second word, *'consume,'* that said, "To destroy, to level." So the darkness won't be allowed to destroy or flatten you. Because if it is flattened there's been total destruction. Then as we look at *'covenant,'* in Deuteronomy we see a promise through Strong's which said, "Choose or choice." Understand this; because He has already chosen you, you are *under the shadow of His wings* for protection. Then it is a choice He made at the cross, trading His life for yours. I tell you we don't begin to understand pain. Lord give us strength to go through it that we might understand the price. I told someone recently I feel like there's five arrows in me. That is pain beyond comprehension. But I must move on, so let's look at *Deuteronomy 8:20* which talks about perishing because we would not be obedient. *"As the nations which the Lord destroyed before your face, so shall ye perish, because ye <u>would not</u> be obedient unto the voice of the Lord your God."* I just saw something for the first time, there is more confirmation about judgement coming to nations that we will see. As it says, *"Before your face."* I tell you the Holy Spirit has given me over one-hundred Scriptures to confirm and clarify about the type of judgement. Even specifics about the enemy. But don't take my word, ask the Holy Spirit to show you what is coming. All because this nation has turned its back on God. Now if you can't get a clear answer, then check Israeli intelligence reports that warns between 6 and 8 cities being hit with nuclear, and if that is not enough, the Lord showed me a Scripture where Ezekiel describes a nuclear blast. Holy Spirit let eyes be opened to this in Jesus Name. Look in *Ezekiel 1:4, "And I looked and behold a whirlwind came out of the north a great cloud and a fire infolding itself, and a brightness was about it and out of the midst there of as the color of amber, out of the midst of the fire."* I tell you in 30 years of study I have never seen this before. Clearly, things that have been hidden since the beginning of time, are being revealed to this generation. Now let's get back to *Deuteronomy 8:20.* I was only directed to research one word, 'perish.' Listen to the words that stood out, "Break, not escape, fall and lose." So we will perish because we broke the covenant made with Him, and we will not be able to escape judgement. But more than that, we will have fallen from grace and the most heartbreaking to Him; we lost our salvation. I'm only going to show you one Scripture to confirm it, even though the Holy Spirit has given dozens of references to walking away. So turn to *Ezekiel 33:13, "When I shall say to the righteous, that he shall surely live; if he trust to his own righteousness and commit iniquity, (becomes a sin lifestyle), all his righteousness shall not be remembered (that's in the lamb's book of life) but for his iniquity that he hath committed he shall die for it,"* (spiritual death). People it's time to wake up and quit following religion, because religion follows ritual that brings death to the spirit. Is that what you want? No conviction, only fleshly comfort. But you must hate where you are at before change can come. So cry out to Him, He is waiting to hear your voice. Lord look down from heaven and see those who are searching for life. Hear the cry of their heart that is my prayer, AMEN. Then when we look at this next Scripture, we find that the remnant are quick to obey. Look at *Samuel 22:45, "Strangers shall submit themselves unto me; as soon as they hear they shall be obedient unto me."* But why are they quick to obey? They are serious about serving. He asks, "What about you, are you quick to follow my Spirit?" I think of Abraham when he was commanded to offer his son Isaac in *Genesis 22*, where we find out that Abraham did not procrastinate when given a directive from the Lord. Look at verse 3, *"And Abraham rose up early in the morning and saddled his ass and took two of his young men with him and Isaac his son and clave the wood for the burnt offering and rose up and went unto the place of which God had told him."* The Spirit leads me to talk about this verse. Why would he take two young men with him? Why not two old and wise? Because Abraham would have needed help if his son ran. I also picture one young man on each side of him as they help this broken man walk down the mountain after he had offered his son. But there is more: Why would we be told he "clave" the wood? Because of splitting the wood it would burn hotter and faster so that his son would have to suffer less agony. That is the mercy and grace of a true father. Now let's return to *2 Samuel 22:45* where we research one word, *'Stranger.'* Strong's has two words we will look at, "Newcomer and outsider." Holy Spirit continue to guide me. "Newcomer" in Webster's said, "one who has lately come to a place or situa-

41

tion." Do you see that's a place of such brokenness that they cry out, not even knowing if God is real or if He really cares? Like a family who has just lost a young son or daughter to disease or tragic death through an auto accident. But not just one child but three. I'm speaking to someone right now. All their love and ability was not able to save the child from death. All the earthly doctors could not help, because even they did not know to look to the great physician Jesus Christ. *Who is able to do exceedingly above and beyond what we could think or even imagine.* I tell you people are looking for answers as never before, because they see the world has given them a false hope. But Jesus says, *"Look to me I will not fail."* Even now I hold on to that truth that He will not fail: for I had to let go of a lady that stole my heart. Meaning I had to wash my hands of her and move on. So is being obedient worth it? Sometimes I wonder; How broken do I have to be before He says, "It is enough?" So don't think the revelation He's given to me has come from easy street, it's been anything but. I even cried out recently to Him to take me home, because I can't handle any more pain. I need to stop for a moment and get quiet before him… (2 hours later). Does that show you where my heart is at? The world doesn't own me, He does. So use the time wisely that has been given to you. Now don't forget what the subject is about in *2 Samuel*: Quick to hear His voice and respond. We continue as we study the last word under strangers: *'Outsider.'* Webster's said, "A person who is excluded from some particular party." Holy Spirit guide me. What about a Baptist that's been taught tongues aren't for today, or a Satanist that repents and turns to Jesus? What about atheists who've been shown the light? Then what about a Catholic who sees what real life is and cries out for the Holy Spirit? Are you getting the picture now? It's in reference to a people who long for His life inside them. Tired of being taught how to settle for so much less. Truly "the church fears that which it can't control." That's why the Holy Spirit is welcome in so few churches. They don't want you to have freedom. But you long for it, that's why you were directed to this book. Which shows you are remnant looking for answers. Now let's continue with *Proverbs 25:12*, which has hidden truth.

"As an earring of gold and an ornament of fine gold, so is a wise reprover upon an obedient ear." For this verse we'll research, "Earring, gold, ornament, fine, reprover and ear." Holy Spirit guide and reveal. Receive as the research connects truth. "As a jewel that shines as a polished and conditioned piece, so is a skillful judge of spirit obedient to listen." Do you see we are that jewel? But we only shine after the pressure is put on us and then finished through the work of the Holy Spirit. Bringing out the beauty that is in us, where His glory can be seen. I so felt the Spirit when I wrote that, I started to cry. Now let me ask a question; Are you willing to let Him put that kind of pressure on you? I would advise not to be quick to answer that question, because the price may be greater than what you are willing to pay. Even now I am holding back the tears. But I must trust Him even in the pain. Thank you Holy Spirit, now this next one, we find that there must be true surrender, even a longing to do His will. Look at *Isaiah 1:19*, *"If ye be willing and obedient, ye shall eat the good of the land."* Again, when specific words are researched as "Willing, good, land and eat," The Word comes alive. Listen: When you breathe after Him, you can rest and be content that He's moving in your behalf. Even

43

feeding you the best meat during the dark night of the soul. Where you are reminded, *"He will give you beauty for ashes,"* and joy where sadness once ruled and reigned. I know He's speaking to some hearts right now. But this verse still has one more truth, and that is, it won't matter where you are at, because favor will flow to you from every direction. Favor as you have never seen before. I tell you, that truth I'm receiving as well. So it won't matter where you go, all needs will always be supplied. Are you beginning to see how important it is to operate in obedience? Then when we look at this next verse, it reveals judgement for rebellion. Look with me in *Isaiah 42:24, "Who gave Jacob for a spoil and Israel to the robbers? Did not the Lord, he against whom we have sinned? For they would not walk in His ways, neither were they obedient unto his law."* So here we see two reasons for why the Lord gave them over to wickedness. But there's more, for when I researched *'Jacob'* and *'Spoil'* we find more truth. Follow me as we listen to what Webster's said for "Jacob." "One who takes the place of another." (That's paraphrased) I just saw evolution taking the place of Creation. Then man teaching by his own understanding, instead of leaning on and trusting in the Holy Spirit to guide and direct. In other words, flesh decides what is spirit based on intellect, not revelation by the Spirit. So just because a person has degrees in theology, does not mean he understands or follows the Holy Spirit. Even recently this truth was confirmed where a man said he would go listen to speakers hoping to be fed. But would find out after hearing them, all they had was head knowledge. Isn't that sad? This represents far too many ministers in the body of Christ. It's no wonder that this man referred to them as "Empty Shells."

For they looked like they were full of the Spirit, but in reality had nothing to give. Now let me give a simple truth: If ministers do not ask the Holy Spirit to empower and guide them, don't be surprised if the Spirit impresses you to get up and leave. Because only those who don't rely on themselves will impart the living Word to you. Receive that truth. Now, let's look at the other word in *Isaiah 42:24,* 'Spoil.' But before I share what was shown, I have to say it first looked like there was no hidden truth, because Strong's said nothing that drew you to the Spirit. However things changed when I asked the Holy Spirit to help me, listen to what Webster's said, "To impair the value or quality of." Do you see that's the quality of life the Lord wants you to have? Don't ever settle for less than the fullness of His Spirit. But more than that, you see the importance of protecting you relationship with Him. Even guarding your walk that none would stumble. Such as the devil trying to puff you up with pride and make you think, "I'm someone special." I tell you be careful when praise starts being poured on you, because it's nothing but a setup from darkness to destroy you. For this confirmation we go back to "Spoil" in Webster's that had another definition. Listen to this truth, "To overindulge or over praise, so as to do harm to the character." That is why The Word says, *Humility before wisdom and humility before honor, but a haughty spirit before a fall."* I tell you never take credit for what He alone has done. Also, if you're spoiled, you're used to having your way. Then look what happens as a result, you become tainted, rotten and unfit for use. I'm supposed to take this one step further by researching *'Taint.'* Catch this! "To stain the honor of someone or something." Do you see that someone is the Holy Spirit and the something is the anointing? Ponder that truth.

Now I'm going to speak from my heart for a minute.

"The pain has been so great, I talked about quitting the ministry. Never have I cried so many tears. Especially when I expected to be invited to spend Christmas Eve with friends, or at least Christmas day. But no phone call ever came and I spent them alone. I call this a December from hell. Sure I could have called someone and invited myself over, but that would have been manipulation and I will not do that. So God must have a reason for what He is allowing. I tell you I have a hard time seeing His hand right now. I feel like my heart has been torn to shreds. But I cannot quit, He must have a plan. Even now I'm reminded of a word that was given two months ago that I'm holding onto. Hoping above hope for change. But it's hard when you don't see any signs. I'm sure there is a lot that would agree. But isn't that what faith is about? Being moved by what He says, not what you see. I tell you I'm going to explode when His promise comes to pass. So don't let go people, keep trusting and believing, no matter what you see."

Thank you Holy Spirit for guiding me through that truth. This concludes all the verses in the Old Testament.

New Testament

Now let's look at the new starting with *Acts 6:7, "And the word of God increased; and the number of disciples multiplied in Jerusalem greatly; and a great company of the priests were obedient to the faith."* There's much truth here. First see that God's

Word had freedom to increase. But why? Ministers were walking in obedience to His Spirit and as a result many were trained as powerful tools to be used for His Glory. Then notice God brought supernatural increase in Spirit. How do we know? The anointed ones multiplied, meaning The Church grew spiritually and in numbers. Because whose job is it to draw people to The Church? The Holy Spirit's. But that doesn't mean you do nothing but sit and get fed, you're to compel all His people to come to that place of surrender in Him. Even as the Scripture says in *Luke 14:23*, *"Go out into the highways and hedges and compel them to come in, that my house may be filled."* Now receive as the Spirit reveals truth through researching, "Highways, hedges and compel." Holy Spirit help.

You're to move people to the place that allows them to see they are in need of the Savior. Using wisdom to draw the lost, like telling them, "After church lunch is on me." Nobody would turn down a free meal. But don't just sit during the service, pray and ask the Holy Spirit to open their spirit to receive. Then have answers ready by the Spirit when excuses try to surface as to why they don't want to go. For example, "I have my own time with Him; Why do I need to go to church? Or the famous one we hear, "I have my own beliefs." For that one you must recognize darkness answering. Then look what was key to increase in spirit, verse 6, *"When they had prayed, they laid their hands on them."* Understand they got quiet before the Lord so they would know these were God's choices not man's. Do you see it? This is the time that only those called are to step in and the others are to pray for strength that they would not falter. In other words, they would not waver or hesitate, but would walk in confidence, knowing they were doing the right thing. Am I speaking from experience? Yes, you already can see that clearly through the writing. So if I've been ready to quit; What does that tell you? You better be ready for a hellish battle, because darkness will attack anyway it can. Even now I fight loneliness trying to creep in and the feeling of abandonment. I'm trying to hold on, but I feel like I am losing my grip. So, what do I need? Encouragement not to give up. But not just that, a multitude of prayers being sent to the Father in my behalf. Even now I'm tearing up and asking; Why does it have to be so hard? It seems pain has become my best friend. I think of the Scripture, *"Weeping may endure for a night, but joy comes in the morning."* I tell you I'm ready to see my morning come. But as I've said before, the anointing is increasing though this. But what a way to receive it. Now anybody who's reading this, I would love to meet in person to hear how it ministered to you. Maybe to remind me the tears have not been in vain and challenge me to go deeper with Him, for you know I am not my own, I belong to Him, I've been bought with a price. Lord, let all those be blessed who are reading this. Let's continue with *Romans 15:18, "For I will not dare to speak of any of those things which Christ hath not wrought by me, to make the Gentiles obedient by word and deed."* Holy Spirit continue to guide. I wasn't familiar with this verse, fact is I had to read it 3 times. Why? This Scripture doesn't make a whole lot of sense, but with the Holy Spirit's help it will. Now sit back and receive truth through my researching, "Dare, speak, wrought, gentiles, word and deed." First I'll summarize, then break it down. "How am I going to speak about forgiveness if I haven't done it yet? How am I going to talk about trust, if I haven't learned it? How am I going to understand the pain that was suffered for me, unless I have partaken of it myself? I think of the Scripture, *"Comfort others with the same comfort that you are comforted with."* *(2 Corinthians 1:4)* So don't be quick to say you understand their pain, if you haven't walked in their shoes. Now I'll break it down for you, "I will not boldly preach anything that Christ has not finished and performed in me. Even to cause those searching for real truth to say, it's obvious he's not following doctrine and he wants accountability for what is said. He shares his life unselfishly, for he's not about making a name for himself." I tell you the only thing I want people to remember about me is my love for the Lord. That they would long to come to the place of surrender as I have, by the Power of the Holy Spirit. But it takes brokenness before you'll cry out for Him. Because brokenness breaks the barrier. So, do you want the barrier of religion broken? It can be you know, all it takes is hunger for relationship and hatred for ritual. Hatred? That's a strong word. But doesn't Satan hate righteousness? Just like we should hate deception and darkness. But darkness day to pay is coming, because *God is not mocked.* Now look what's promised from His Word for the remnant. *"Evil shall slay the wicked and they that hate the righteous shall be desolate."* (That's *Psalm 34:21*) Notice it doesn't say the righteous will slay the wicked, so the darkness will turn on itself at that time, even as it happened in The Word. I tell you <u>we must still believe for miracles even when all hope seems lost.</u> Because recently the Spirit spoke and said, *"Is anything too hard for me?"* Sure I know, "He can do all things," but honestly? My hope tank is about empty, I've been blasted out of the water so many times, meaning: Just when hope started rising believing promises to be fulfilled, I would suffer the loss I'd just hoped to gain. It had been like I was on a spiritual roller coaster. Then the tears would start over again. I even told Him recently, "Quit playing games, I've had enough pain." Yes, I said that to the God of this universe. That's getting gut bucket real from your heart. But that's what He's waiting for, a level of honesty about your pain. So don't raise your hands when you want to shake your fist in His face. Haven't you ever just wanted to say, "The hell with you!" or "Don't even try to tell me you love me, for I see no love in this pain." But religion would never dare to say that, because religion is not about surrender, but serving self. Isn't that what the Pharisees did? They served only themselves, wanting to kill anyone who pointed to a different direction than religion. That's why the traditional Catholic Church is dying, their imparting anything but life. How do I know? Because I was born and raised Catholic. Therefore I know what I am talking about. Church, we need to wake up and start following the Spirit. Understand the level of surrender will reveal the depth of anointing that has freedom to flow through you to others. Now this next Scripture goes with what was just spoken about. What is that? Testing. Something we all hate when it comes. But why? We know it's time for our roots to go deeper, and our faith to get stronger. I think of the Scripture found in *1 Peter 4:12, "Beloved think it not strange concerning the fiery trial which is to try you, as though some strange thing happened unto you."* I tell you nobody wants to hear that verse, especially when you are trying so hard to walk right. What's the purpose for this level of suffering? The answer is found in chapter 5 of 1 Peter verse 10, where it says, *"After that ye have suffered awhile, make you perfect, stablish, strengthen, settle you."* As I looked at these words, I wondered; is there hidden truth? Yes, for when all these were researched, it helped me to understand what He was and is doing in each of us. Follow along, *'Perfect'* said in Strong's, "To complete thoroughly, fit, frame, prepare and restore." So He's finishing a work that was started. I think of the Scripture, *"He who has begun a good work will be faithful to complete it."* Then He fits us or puts us in the right position, that will flow with the body. Be it a teacher of The Word, missionary spreading The Word or a prophet that holds them accountable for The Word. Now, *'Frame,'* first He's faming your house to be strong so when the winds of adversity come you'll be able to stand strong. And; Why are you able to stand? The foundation of truth was dug deep. Second, you'll know by the Spirit how to reach the lost by putting in a language truth they can understand. Then you as a servant, prepare hearts to receive revelation that will bring transformation. Bringing them to the place of excitement about the things of the Spirit. But why would they get excited? They're getting set free from religion. Now "Restore," Holy Spirit guide me. You bring those back to the place they once were with Him, where there was a longing to love and serve Him with all their heart. For they now know what is real. I think of the movie "Avatar" where a man sees for the first time, what is real and what is not. For what he thought was life, was nothing but a smoke screen of deception. Because it's not about clothes and cars, but Kingdom. Are you beginning to see how important obedience is? Then let's get more truth as we research "Stablish, strengthen and settle" in *1 Peter 5:10.* When I researched "Stablish," the truth really hit home, listen to what Strong's said, "To turn resolutely in a certain direction." Now receive as truth gets stronger through the definition for "Resolute," catch this, "Characterized by firmness or determination, pursuing a fixed purpose." Do you get this? You must stay focused on what the goal is: winning souls, saving them from a pain that never stops, even suffering, that they might see His hand in helping. I think of the Scripture, *"For thy sake have I borne reproach"* *(Psalms 69:7)* <u>NOTE:</u> This is the second time this is referred to, so it must be important. So this verse makes it clear it's about salvation of souls. Now receive what *'Strengthen'* said, "Confirm in spiritual knowledge and power." So it's knowledge that will set the captives of religion free and take those that are His to new heights in spirit. But what's the *'Power'* in reference to? Setting the demon possessed free! Through the anointing that comes from a surrendered life. But wait, that's not all, "Strengthen" also said, "To stand, abide, appoint, continue and establish." So you're to stand for righteousness, abide in His presence, appoint those to their calling, continue your journey growing with Him and establish a firm foundation that cannot be shaken. Then *'Settle,'* that's issues you've struggled with for many years, not knowing what to believe, because truth has been twisted for far too long, confusing the saints of God. But no more, for it's time for change, moving from flesh to spirit. This is confirmed when we see what else "settle" said, catch this, "To restore calmness or comfort." So it's time for the peace to be restored to your spirit. I tell you I'm ready to receive the peace that surpasses understanding. I tell you I need a word from Him as never before, to comfort and encourage. So hungry to be fed, but no place to go. For far too many churches have their own agendas, meaning their own ideas about what people need. It's no wonder why former churchers want nothing to do with the church. But you won't see it, until you get sick of ritual. I tell you He cries out for a spotless bride. Now before I go on to the next Scripture,

I'm to tell you the greatest lesson I'm learning through the pain and tears, Trust, something we all must grow in. He reminds me of the Scripture, *"Trust in the Lord with all thine heart and lean not unto thine own understanding. (Proverbs 3:5)."* I tell you it's easy to read, but tough to follow. So if a minister struggles, don't be so hard on yourself, because we all need to trust Him more. Now another verse about testing found in *2 Corinthians 2:9, "For to this end also did I write that I might know the proof of you, whether ye be obedient in all things."*

Testing; Don't you hate it? Even I said to the Lord one day, "You know my heart; Why?" He said, "I'm testing the faith in you," only now do I see why faith must be tested, we must be established in our belief that His promises are true. Even when everything speaks to the contrary, or should we say the opposite of what we're believing for. Lord, help us to trust when we don't know what's going on. Help us to believe that Your promises are true, even when it seems there is no hope. I tell you it's easier to give up than stand. But do you know what will be gained as a result of this? A new level of faith. Has He given you a vision for a promise? Then hold on to it. But if He hasn't, ask Him to give you one, that your faith might be strengthened, even as I'm asking for it now. Time to return to *2 Corinthians 2:9*, where we will research two words, "Know and Proof." Continue to guide me Holy Spirit. Several words showed up under *'Know,'* "allow, be aware, feel, perceive, be resolved, be sure and understand." First, He allows darkness to invade our lives that we might be made aware where we're weak. To feel His pain for the lost and hurting. Then to perceive that there's areas in our lives that need work, like learning the importance of speaking His promises back to Him, even in the midst of battle. To recognize through the testing or trial, we are now responding to problems or difficulties differently than before. Knowing tears don't move Him, but faith does. I am reminded of the Scripture, *"Without faith it's impossible to please God."* Then to become resolved in our thinking. Meaning, we've made the decision where we're going to stand with Him firmly fixed in our purpose to serve Him. That we would be sure of our calling and confident as He takes us forward by His Spirit. Then to understand that He's using these trials that He might be glorified through them. That He's burning the flesh away, that His Spirit would have freedom to operate from within. Are you getting the picture now? He wants to answer the cry of our heart that longs to heal and deliver from darkness all those who are searching for Him. I tell you He wants to be found for all of us, that none would perish. He reminds me of the Scripture found in *2 Peter 3:9, "Not willing that any should perish but that all should come to repentance."* I tell you, this is the cry of the remnant. Now let's look at the second word in 2 Corinthians *'Proof.'* Again, Strong's gives several words, let's see which ones speak to your spirit. "Test, experience, trial, acceptable, approved and tried." Isn't it interesting the first word is test? So He's watching to see what will raise up in us, fear or faith. Then as I looked at the word test, my spirit started stirring that there's something hidden here, but what was it? Get ready for what each letter stood for: <u>T-trusting E-every S-set T-trial.</u> Ponder that truth. So; Are we trusting Him? No, not for a lot of Christians. We want to trust, but not when we don't see any reason to. For many of us we know the promises are true, but are they really mine to keep? Are they for today, or did they die with the Old Testament church as many teach? Only you can answer that, telling people not one of His promises have failed. But religion doesn't want to hear that, for they've made up their mind what is real. Then we're to experience what it is to be betrayed by someone you love. Can you imagine what Jesus felt, knowing that Judas was going to betray Him? I can, now that I've experienced it. You're stunned, numb, struggling to believe it really happened. Yet is there bitterness and resentment? No, only love. But you wouldn't understand this unless you went through it. Then when we look at *'Trial'* we find another truth that was hidden. Listen: <u>T-test R-required I-in A-are (our) L-life.</u> So the trial must come if we're to grow in Him. He even sees them as something precious in His sight. Do you believe that? You will now through this Scripture in *1 Peter 1:7*, *"That the trial of your faith being much more precious than of gold that perishes, through it be tried with fire might be found unto praise and honor and glory at the appearing of Jesus Christ."* I see Jesus smiling at Father God as He watches how you're looking to Him for answers to carry you through till the victory comes. I tell you I'm crying out for answers, looking to Him as never before. Yet this is acceptable in His sight? Yes, because He already sees what the result will be. So it's allowed and even approved of by the Father. For <u>the Father sees what the pain will produce in your life. Lord, show what You're producing in me,</u> because the tears have blurred my vision. Do you hear the pain I'm crying out to be set free from? Truly there's no suffering I couldn't relate to. Now the last word *'Tried.'* For this one, I was impressed to research all the different reference numbers. So see if any

Scriptures, ideas or insight come as they're read, "Fuse, re-fine, melt, purge away, examine, prove, tempt, endeavor, scrutinize, entice, discipline, allow, discern, and be on fire." Holy Spirit illuminate those you want spoken about. We start with *'Fuse'* - Webster's had this truth that stood out, "To become mixed or united by or as if by melting together." I see two things here, first we're becoming mixed with His Spirit through the fellowship of pain. We're also becoming more like Him, seeing the lost and hurting as He does, with great compassion. Now a truth He wants me to share, He said one day, "One of the reasons drugs are so rampant, there's many people trying to escape the pain they carry in-side and since the world won't point them to Me, they try to escape from reality their way." He said, "Drugs are out of control because the world is not about to tell them I AM is the answer." Now the second truth about *'fuse'* revealed by the Spirit, this is also in reference to the husband and wife that become melted together as they seek His Kingdom for answers, when the battle becomes intense. So through this they're learning to operate as one with His Spirit. Because if it's fused, they're being melted together by His Spirit, and that's a bond which can never be broken. Next we look at *'Purge away.'* Webster's said, "Free from impurities and to rid of sin, guilt or defilement." Do you see He wants to re-move contaminated thinking? Just like yesterday a thought came to me that was so disgusting, I cried out to the Lord to remove it from my mind. I tell you, it was from the pits of hell itself. Do you see why we must be refined? The heat or trial brings the impurities to the surface that they might be shown and then removed. Thus making us a purer vessel for His Spirit to flow through. That is if you want to be used for His Glory. Then He asks for you to "Examine yourself; Is it pleasing to Him? Do you manipulate to get, or surrender to give?" I tell you The Church has taught us how to manipulate long enough! Do you hear the cry of the Father? He wants change. Will you help it to come about? People, this is His heart, He weeps over what His bride has become. But only the remnant cry with Him, only they see it as He does. Then when I saw the word 'Prove,' two truths were revealed again. See if you catch it. "To establish the truth," that's in your heart, so circumstances won't shake you. Am I speaking from experience? You already know that answer. Then Webster's said, "To establish the authenticity." That's the realness of your walk with Him that others might see and know our Jesus is real. This was confirmed when the Spirit impressed me to research "Authenticate." Listen to this: "To establish as worthy of belief." So the world needs to see that our Jesus is very much alive. That even the worst critic that "scrutinizes" to the enth degree, will not be able to deny the power of our living God. Such as a miracle healing that takes place before their very eyes. A miracle that cannot be explained away. Like an arm growing out where a stub was before. I tell you that will get the world's attention. The Spirit impresses me to share a truth that I cried out to know for many years. It has to do with the Scripture found in *John 14:12, "Greater works than these shall He do, because I go to the Father."* Have you ever wondered what the "greater works" are? What could we do that was greater than what Jesus did? Yet the word is clear we'll do them. So what's this in reference to? Get ready; the Lord said, "Brian I did no creative miracles, yes I took a shriveled arm and made it whole and I put an ear back on. But I didn't grow legs out where stubs were before. That is only the beginning of the greater works you'll do for my Glory." So what kind of surrender do you think needs to be made to Him for that level of anointing to flow through us? Yet the remnant will pay the price. Now let's look at *Ephesians 6:5*, *"Servants be obedient to them that are your masters according to the flesh, with fear and trembling, in singleness of your heart as unto Christ."* For this verse we'll research three words, "servants, masters and singleness." First a truth about servants. A true servant always knows what the will of the Master is. How? Because of time spent with Him, for he knows His voice and His heart. Also, a true servant has no problem following leadership led by His Spirit. Then when *'Masters'* was researched we find their teachings line up with The Word of God and followed by those who hear it. Now let's look at *'Singleness,'* which gave us a load of truths through Strong's. "Sincerity, not self-seeking, generosity, bountifulness and simplicity." Holy Spirit guide. We will not represent Him falsely, but with honesty and purity will we operate. We won't get entangled with irrelevant matters through religious people who would try to sidetrack us from the real issue. Then we have a willingness to give our lives in every area for the Gospel's sake, even giving unselfishly to further The Kingdom. We have an abundance of His Word in our spirit always willing to give it out when directed by Him. Now let's look at *'Simplicity.'* I think of not being veiled to true believers. So nothing is hidden for those who hunger for Him. Then when I looked in Webster's it revealed promises and decisions we all need to remember. For Webster's said, "Absence of complexity, intricacy and artificiality." So it's an absence of exaggerated concern or fear, but more than just that, no more confusion because we're flowing with the Spirit. Then the biggie: We won't follow or walk in laws made by man. Amen. I tell you man's rules and laws have kept God's people in bondage long enough. Do you see it's time for the religious captives to be set free? I tell you I'm sick of religion, because religion will keep you from relationship. Then I ran across a word I wasn't familiar with, *'Stilted.'* That truly represents too many ministers today. Because listen to what Webster's said, "Artificially dignified, formal or pompous." Do you see too many leaders have exalted themselves? It's not about position or status, but sensitivity to what He wants to accomplish through a surrendered vessel. Now receive confirmation what God sees through one word "Pompous," "Exaggerated show of dignity, self-importance in speech and manner." What's happened to us? Where are the leaders that walked in humbleness of heart? They became arrogant, proud and focused on building their kingdom, not His. Do you see it? I said to a group recently: Show me one church where signs, wonders and miracles are taking place. Do you hear the cry of His heart? He wants the captives free. Now receive the truth in Simplicity in Ephesians, "Remnant, be obedient to the teachers of truth according to the spirit of Christ that dwells in you. Walk with a reverential fear of the God you serve, remembering it's not about you, but Him in you." Thank you Holy Spirit for your guidance. Now let's continue in truth as we research *Philippians 2:8, "And being found in fashion as a man he humbled himself and became obedient unto death even the death of the cross."* As I studied this Scripture, it became clear this verse is in reference to Jesus giving His life through obedience to the Father. But what's the hidden truth? It comes about when two words are researched, "Found and Fashion". Found said, "Get, obtain, perceive and see." Can you tell which word held the answer? You will after we research "Fashion" in Strong's, listen: "Possession, ability, contiguity, relation and condition." Now let's put it together by the Spirit. We start with the definition for *'Perceive,'* Webster's said, "To take notice of, observe, detect." I think of the Scripture in *Acts 4:13, "Now when they saw the boldness of Peter and John, and perceived that they were unlearned and ignorant men, they marveled and they took knowledge (or notice of) of them that they had been with Jesus."* Question; Can people tell there is something different about you that they are drawn to? Do they sense a peace in you that they long for? If they do, then you are walking with Him. But how do you show people the source of your peace? By asking the Father to open doors and give you divine appointments wherever you go. Like the grocery store for instance, the ideal place to display Christ. You know like when you are in the check-out lane and you hear the same broken record over and over; How are you? Then as always your same response, "Fine." Which is most of the time a lie. So break your recording and get real. How? By breaking their routine and giving a response that stops them in their tracks. Like I did recently when I responded "I'm growing." First she looked at me and then said, "How can you be growing?" Then I almost laughed when she commented, "You are too old." To which I replied, "I'm growing in the Holy Spirit." Do you know when I said that she perked up and came alive? Then I shared what the Holy Spirit gave to me, handed her a ministry card and left. Now; Don't you think she will remember me the next time I come in? Of course she will and maybe even open up and share her heart. That's the way we reach people being real, not slapping them with a Scripture, but instead being that living epistle they can read. Now let's do our research starting with 'Possession,' Webster's said, "To have as a quality or characteristic." Do you see we're to have the qualities of Christ operating in our lives? Like honesty and integrity that people see we walk in and excellence that we strive for, with a reputation that is respected. Then when I saw the word 'ability,' it came to me the ability to hear from the Spirit because of the surrendered walk. But not just that, being able to perform tasks others wouldn't touch, such as laying hands on a leper, something many wouldn't do because of fear. Now 'Contiguity,' a word I never heard before. So we look to Webster's that says, "Sharing an edge." The first thing that comes to mind is sharing insight that came by the Spirit and revelation given through the Spirit. Again, I'm to give an example revealed by the Holy Spirit. When The Word said, *"He had no place to lay His head,"* it wasn't in reference to sleep, but leadership, something that is lacking sorely.

So, what is it going to take for The Church to change? True repentance, something they don't think is needed, but you do as His remnant. You see what they can't or won't. I think of the handwriting on the wall that appeared after Nebuchadnezzar started praising the gods of gold and silver. I tell you the handwriting is on the wall for God's judgement and The Church can't see it. Do you see how far we've fallen? It's so sad. Why did we go back to religion? Because comfort became more important than conviction. Now let's look at 'Relation' the last word we'll research under 'Fashion.'

First I'm to ask; What is your relationship with Him? Do you still love Him or have you turned your back on Him? Have you walked away because of pain you couldn't comprehend? What about battles that seemed futile to fight? What about prayers that were prayed with many tears, that seemed to go no higher than the ceiling? It's no wonder why so many have walked away. Because even when you turned to The Church for answers, they had a deaf ear to your cry, not even caring you were dying on the inside. How many could relate to what was just said? I believe more than you ever thought possible. Do you hear His heart through these words? He wants His spotless bride back. Now hear the simple truth of *Philippians 2:8*, "You were perceived by many to be in possession of His Spirit, then the ability to operate with Him by the Spirit and then teach others how to be victorious through His Spirit.

Thank you Holy Spirit, continue to guide. So it must be evident in our life that we know Him, and be consistent in the walk with Him, that others might see and want what we have. I tell you everything in our life should point to Him. But how do we know when people want what we have? One way is when you see respect being shown. Like I saw recently at a carry-out pizza place, where one of the workers called me by name and said your order is ready. Do you see he wanted to connect? And he did, for I gave a big smile in response. Then another man said, "We need more people like you." I tell you those little statements go a long way when you are ready to give up. So is all the pain worth it? Yes, for yesterday the Lord told me to go have breakfast at a specific restaurant and impressed me to invite a friend to join me, Then in the course of speaking with him he saw someone who needed help coming in, so I started talking to the people in the booth behind me. I tell you it was a Holy Ghost set up! For all of a sudden I looked at this man's wife and my spirit was deeply stirred. So I asked the man if I could pray for his wife, he says yes without hesitation. Now watch what the Holy Gost does. The Spirit makes it clear she is in pain, so I ask, "Where is the pain in your back?" I find the spot, start praying, and then get a word of knowledge that it's a pinched nerve and that she had just experienced a spasm that froze her. Then the Spirit said, "It's an injury." So I tell her what I heard, she then responds, "I was injured at work." The Spirit does not release me from praying so I continue. Then I ask, "Has the pain lessened?" She says, "Yes." So I continue to pray, then I'm told to stop and she says, "The pain is gone." So is it worth it? Yes, so trust what He's accomplishing through the pain in your own life. It is worth every tear. Thank you Lord for using me for your Glory. Now turn to *Titus 2:5*, but we will start with verse 4 to receive understanding about the subject. Leaders teaching women to respect and love their family, walking as godly women honoring Him. So let's look at verse 4, *"That they (the leaders) may teach the young women to be sober, to love their husbands, to love their children."* Now verse 5, *"To be discreet, chaste, keepers at home, good, obedient to their own husbands, that The Word of God be not blasphemed."* So here we see the leader's responsibility to teach women the importance of living a righteous life. Now see all the areas that God wants them operating in through researching. "Discreet, chaste, keepers and blasphemed." I'll rewrite the verse with the revelation that was given by the Spirit. "Leaders are to teach women to be honest, frank and candid, meaning without prejudice and fair. Then they're free from dirt, stains, and impurities and unsoiled. In other words free from sin or a sin lifestyle with no immoral ways that their conduct shows they walk with a stricter set of rules following The Word of God. Free from disgrace and defilement. Then they see the evil for what it is, darkness trying to entice." Such as, "If you were working people would see your gifts and talents, because your husband doesn't appreciate all the things you do. Then; Wouldn't you like to have a nicer car and what about your clothes, isn't it time you got some new ones? Maybe some that shows your beauty, because your husband doesn't even compliment you any more, even when you've tried to look attractive and sexy for him." These are just the things the devil will speak to women when men start taking their wives for granted. Then leaders are to show women how to let their words be few and well chosen, that others would see the blessing for walking with a surrendered heart. The Holy Spirit just reminded me of Proverbs 31, which praises women of God. Specifically verse 26, *"She openeth her mouth with wisdom and her tongue is the law of kindness."* These are the kind of women The Church should be raising up. Church, do you see how much needs to change? I think of the Laodicean church in *Revelation 3:15, "I know thy works that thou art neither cold nor hot. So then, because thou art lukewarm, and neither cold or hot, I will spew thee out of my mouth."* Now look at The Church's arrogance in verse 17, *"Because thou sayest I am rich and increased with goods and have need of nothing and knowest not that thou art <u>wretched</u> and <u>miserable</u> and <u>poor</u> and <u>blind</u> and <u>naked</u>."* Now receive what the Lord was saying after the words underlined were researched.

First, you are living in degradation, meaning you've lost your worth. Then things that you use to stand strong in, or against, you've now found compromise for. Like abortion issues and homosexuality, things you wouldn't dare speak out against. Lest you offend some in your church. Before I go on, the Lord said to me recently, "One of the reasons why the churches aren't growing is they won't deal with issues inside the church." I confirm this through a woman that had my Corvette keyed by an accomplice while it was in the parking lot. But what did I do to deserve that kind of treatment? Nothing. Then I asked the Holy Spirit who did it and why. First He said through a Prophet, "Two people did the deed." Then I asked, "Why?" He said, "It was because of jealousy." So only after I received confirmation did I tell the Pastor, "This woman must be dealt with." I even gave the Prophet's name who could be contacted to confirm what was said. Then later I called the Prophet to ask if the Pastor had called. He said he'd never heard from him. Then after about four months, the Holy Spirit gave me a word to text to the Pastor that judgement would now fall if this wasn't dealt with. In response all he said in a text was, "Quit talking like this!" I then responded, "This is not me but the Holy Spirit Who gave this warning." I then was told he would see me after the New Year. But as I'm sure you've guessed, I've never heard a word from him. So as you see, I'm speaking from experience. Now there is one thing I did for accountability, I contacted a Prophet and told him what the Holy Spirit had told me to say to this minister. Do you see how hard I'm trying to walk right? One more thing, this is the same Prophet who got the word of knowledge two people were involved in the vandalism done to my car. One more thing, this Prophet has known me about 30 years and is almost 90 years old. So he knows the Spirit's Voice. Now let's get back to Revelations and see what else the Lord wants to say to us through the Laodicean church. Holy Spirit continue to guide. He says, "Where's my joy? Where is the character of Christ you're to show to all those who are searching for truth? Where is the excellence in spirit? Where is the fear of God? Where is your moral standing? You are poor in spirit and don't even know it and you no longer hunger and thirst for my righteousness." He says, "My people have increased with pride, conceit, selfishness, coldness, bitterness, unforgiveness and lies. My people have left themselves defenseless, vulnerable and open to harm because they came out from under my wings of protection." Are you hearing this Church? This is the Father's heart that cries out for you to return to Him.

Now before I go on to the next Scripture, He wants me to speak His heart. He said, "The churches in Revelation represent all the problems that are evident and operating in my house today." So study Revelations and see the things that must be corrected if The Church is to grow. Now let's look at another verse in Titus 2 and see what the Spirit is saying. Only this time I'm going to write it without man's words added. *"Servants be obedient unto your own masters, to please well in all not answering again."* He leads me to research three words, "Servant, masters and again." Now let's rewrite it with the revelation added, "remnant, be knit together with my Spirit. Listen to the teachers that I've put before you, trusting that which they're speaking is coming through my Spirit. So stand the ground that I've given to you, and come against those who would try to deny or dispute what you know is true." Thank you Holy Spirit for your guidance. He just reminded me of the Scripture found in *2 Timothy 2:15, "Study to show thyself approved unto God, a workman that needeth not to be ashamed, rightly dividing the word of truth."* I tell you, only by the Spirit can it be done. Now let's see what the Lord wants to say to us through *1 Peter 1:14.* But for clarity's sake, I'm going to paraphrase it a little, *"Obedient children don't fashion yourselves to the former lusts in your ignorance."* For this Scripture I've researched, "Children, fashion, lusts and ignorance." Now receive a simple and easy to understand truth as I write it by His Spirit, "You that are my sons and daughters that I bought with a price. Don't be quick, ready and willing to covet those thing that are the desires of the flesh and then act as if you didn't know what my Word said, for I will not accept this when I judge you for turning your back on me." Don't play games people, for God is serious when it comes to rebellion. *"For rebellion is as the sin of witchcraft."* So this verse in *1 Samuel 15:23* shows that rebellion and witchcraft operate on the same level of wickedness working <u>with</u> darkness. For when I researched *'Witchcraft'* the word *'Sorcery'* came up that said, "The use of supernatural power over others <u>through the assistance of evil spirits.</u> So run from rebellion. Thank you Lord for the truths You've revealed by your Spirit. May what they've read go deep inside and stay. Now before we close this book, the Holy Spirit said, "Research the word "Remnant." So prepare your spirit for a download from Him. Remnant will always <u>extend</u> a helping hand, then be challenged to <u>stretch</u> their faith. They will remind you of promises in His Word like, *"He is able to do <u>exceedingly abundantly</u> above all that we could ask or think according to the power of the Holy Spirit working in us."* Then we <u>excel</u> in the things of the Spirit and as a result, we <u>abound</u> with blessings. We're learning what it means to <u>rest</u> in Him and trust. But; How are we to rest?

By receiving what the letters stand for:

R – Restore the relationship to what it once was with Him.

E – Encourage others (and yourself) not to grow weary while well doing,

S – Speak His Word, and then the biggie,

T – Trust His timing.

Something we all struggle with. Now let's continue, remnant know they're going to be <u>persecuted</u> for <u>pursuing</u> holiness and righteousness. But that doesn't stop them from *preaching <u>deliverance</u> to the captives.* Then show them there is a way of <u>escape</u> from the sin they are bound to through Jesus Christ. Then the remnant aren't interested in earthly <u>rewards</u>, but heavenly ones. For their treasures are not of this world.

Thank you Holy Spirit for all the truths you've revealed. Bless every page of this word that He may be glorified in it. AMEN!

COMING SOON

3 NEW Books by Prophet and Teacher Brian Ohse

- The HEART CRY of The Father

- The Keys to Unlocking
THE DOOR OF VICTORY

- WALK BY FAITH, and not by sight
[Volumes 1 & 2]